EMOTIONAL EATING WORKBOOK

A Complete Guide To Stop Emotional Eating, Binge, Overeating, and Obesity through the proposal of multidisciplinary therapeutic strategies

By

Sara Williams

Table of Contents

1. INTRODUCTION

Obesity is a complex disease, which requires an integrated, interdisciplinary approach and, possibly, adapted from time to time to the needs of the individual patient. At the basis of this pathology, there is often the presence of dysfunctional eating behavior. Eating disorders have for some years been the subject of increasing attention by the scientific world and the community of health and social workers, due to their spread among younger sections of the population and their multifactorial etiology.

Data from the World Health Organization underline that 86% of deaths and 75% of health expenditure in Europe and USA are caused by chronic diseases, which have as the lowest common denominator 4 main risk factors: smoking, alcohol abuse, poor diet, and physical inactivity. The latter two conditions are the basis of the alarming and continuous increase in the prevalence of overweight and obesity in Western and developing populations, which has reached the proportions of an unstoppable epidemic. Overweight and obesity in Europe are responsible for about 80% of cases of type 2 diabetes, 55% of cases of hypertension, and 35% of cases of ischaemic heart disease, resulting in 1 million deaths per year and 12 million patients per year. The recommendation to reduce body weight when high is based on evidence of the relationship between obesity and lower life expectancy. However, long-term treatment is very problematic and requires an integrated approach, using the tools available in a complementary way, using different professional skills, which share the same therapeutic objective. In this regard, treatment increasingly involves clinical psychology, psychiatry, and the internal branches of medicine. In the framework of a multidimensional clinical approach to complete and integrate this therapeutic strategy, numerous studies have demonstrated the effectiveness of physical activity in subjects with obesity in comorbidities with an eating disorder. Detecting the presence of this disorder can optimize the motor type program.

2. Food and emotional needs

Why are we eating?

In the area of eating behavior, what happens is that food needs do not always coincide with emotional needs.

To stay alive, our body "uses calories" (the ones we introduce with food). It is called the basal metabolism and it is the basic energy consumption that our body uses to stay "alive". We do not control it and it does not depend on our will.

What depends on our will is the choice of food, the quantity, the willingness to engage in physical activity. We can control this.

If we use more calories than we eat, or if we give up the calories we eat, then we can achieve results in weight reduction over time.

If we limit foods that are harmful to our health, such as celiac disease, diabetes, hypercholesterolemia, we will have better management of the disease.

Many factors affect our weight and diet. If you belong to the "dieter" category (people who have done a lot of dieting) you know the concept of calories, metabolism, and much more. You also know the importance of physical activity, but it is not only by finding time to exercise or by choosing a salad instead of a cheeseburger - certainly a praiseworthy and healthy decision - that your situation will change.

Food professionals indicate 5 elements to consider when changing your eating style:

1. Choice of food

2. Food knowledge

3. Condiments used and cooking systems

4. Amount of food ingested

5: Awareness

The first four points refer to HOW you eat, WHAT you eat, and HOW much you eat. Too often, however, the factor of AWARENESS (WHY and HOW you eat) is overlooked.

Understanding the last factor can transform the effectiveness of a diet (in the short term) into a lasting change in habits, i.e. a change in lifestyle.

Having a healthy lifestyle does not mean changing one's whole life but making small, progressive changes that stabilize over time.

Food and emotions

Food has always been our interest. We eat out of hunger, we eat at parties. We fast to honor a religious precept. We celebrate our birthdays with food. We offer food to our guests.

We associate food with social and emotional events that have nothing to do with hunger. What about "comfort food"?

These are foods that help us to deal with difficult situations. Foods that comfort us. Foods that remind us of good times in our past and help us to face a difficult present.

It happens, so, to eat without being really hungry. Imagine this behavior repeated over time. Let's imagine that it can happen several times a day. What happens if we eat without hunger?

Before we continue, it is important to understand what hunger is:

HUNGER IS THE FEELING YOU GET WHEN A SERIES OF SIGNALS, COMING FROM OUR BODY, INFORM US THAT WE ARE "SHORT OF FUEL" (ENERGY).

If we eat without hunger, we get fat!

Most people who have problems with excess body weight eat without hunger.

It is important to make a distinction between eating out of necessity, that is to say, out of a lack of calories and natural needs, and eating out of an emotional urge, that is, based on states of mind that, over the years, we have learned to combine with food, but that has nothing to do with a biological need.

Generally, we do not ask ourselves why we breathe or how to regulate our heart rate. They are automatic behaviors.

Eating and drinking, on the other hand, are partly voluntary acts.

When we drink water we do not think to solve internal conflicts, reduce stress, but only that our body is dehydrated and has the need to introduce liquids. When we think about food, instead, we assume that eating is a totally voluntary act and, as such, completely conscious.

OUR EATING HABITS ARE INFLUENCED BY THE EMOTIONS

Several scientific studies have shown that, within 24 hours, we experience more than 41 emotions ranging from joy, frustration, boredom, anxiety, etc.. It is not surprising, therefore, to know that some emotions affect our diet.

So, we can find: the "emotional eaters" who know they are and say so, think that it will be too difficult to solve the situation, and then continue to do what they must not do: eat to "distract" themselves from the emotions they feel.

They live in the vicious circle of trying to control what they eat and, if they don't, they depress themselves because they don't see results on the scale. At best, they start a new diet again or decide to "let go of the food".

Emotional eaters" who, on the other hand, do not know they are, are often to a greater extent and think that behind their failures there is some problem that hinders weight loss. They have many beliefs and among the most widespread we find:

- • The belief that you have a "slow metabolism".
- • The certainty of being a victim of a hormonal problem.
- • Hope we have the thyroid asleep.

Behind these beliefs hides a desire: that a pill, a drug, a surgery will solve the problem. An attitude that is not only responsible but also a lack of awareness.

Our body weight increases because we eat too much, that is, you eat more calories than you burn!

We use calories when we move. That's why exercise is important for weight loss so and bring other health benefits (in the case of diabetes, for example, helps regulate insulin).

ARE YOU AN EMOTIONAL EATER?

We don't always eat to satisfy hunger. Instead, we turn to food to obtain comfort food, to reduce stress, or to find relief from boredom, anxiety, and anger. In general, food is a source of well-being. Good, available at all times, easy to obtain, not particularly harmful.

THERE IS NO BETTER SOLUTION THAN FOOD WHEN WE WANT TO "COMPENSATE" FOR NEGATIVE EMOTIONS.

This behavior is called "emotional eating" and is an eating behavior in which food is used to make us feel better; eating to fill emotional "gaps" rather than to fill the stomach.

It often happens without our awareness and automatically.

UNFORTUNATELY, "EMOTIONAL EATING" DOES NOT SOLVE OUR EMOTIONAL PROBLEMS; ON THE CONTRARY, IT USUALLY WORSENS THEM.

Not only does the negative emotion remain but, in addition to this, we feel guilty for having eaten "too much" or for having eaten things that are not necessary or even harmful.

Learning to recognize the emotion that triggers the behavior of emotional eating is the first step to manage this addiction to food and change the habits that have sabotaged your diets in the past.

Let's be clear: using food, occasionally, to feel better, is not in itself a bad thing. When, however, it happens often and every time you are angry, tired, disappointed the first impulse is to open the refrigerator, then it is necessary to understand the reasons for this behavior and remedy it.

Research has shown that obese people tend to eat to control negative emotions. The more they gain weight, the more this behavior increases.

Also, in many cases, food is used when the person does not know how to define the negative feeling he or she feels. In other words, it is eaten when the negative emotion is not "labeled".

Eating may make you feel better on the spot, but immediately afterward, the negative feeling you were looking for reappears.

The emotions of anger, loneliness, anxiety, which have given the stimulus to look for food, are still there. And there is another problem: unnecessary calories make the needle of the scale go up and harmful foods create a deterioration of health parameters.

First of all, then, it is important to understand the motivation that leads to eating: emotions or need for food?

At this point it is necessary to distinguish between physical and emotional hunger:

PHYSICAL HUNGER

It is the signal that intervenes to warn us that the body (brain, muscles, internal organs) is running out of fuel (remember the metaphor of the car?). If we do not want to end the trip with the car stationary in the middle of the road, we must provide for finding a petrol pump and .... EAT!

Physical Hunger intervenes when there is an energy deficit in the body and is, therefore, a signal that requires the introduction of carbohydrates, fats, and proteins, to meet this need.

EMOTIONAL HUNGER

Emotional hunger, on the other hand, is a type of hunger that comes when situations or thought processes give rise to a "desire for food" and not because of a real energy deficit.

This is how it happens that when we eat for Emotional Hunger we eat unconsciously because we do not realize that what we need is not food but for something else.

EMOTIONAL HUNGER PHYSICAL HUNGER

EMOTIONAL HUNGER	PHYSICAL HUNGER
Starts suddenly.	Starts gradually.
Felt mostly in your head or on the surface of your thoughts.	Physically felt within your stomach.
A sharp craving that tends to be incessant.	A growling pang that tends to come in waves.
You become fixated on a specific food, taste, or texture.	You are open to many options, including less palatable foods.
Hard to satisfy, often leads to eating until uncomfortably full.	Easy to satisfy with a normal amount of food.
May trigger feelings of guilt, self-loathing, regret, or shame.	Doesn't make you feel bad about yourself.

Emotional Hunger can manifest itself with high intensity and that is why it is easy to make mistakes and confuse it with Physical Hunger. Here are the main differences:

- Emotional hunger comes suddenly. In a few moments, we feel we have to eat. And we have to do it now! Even if we had eaten a little earlier, we feel the urgency to eat again.
- Emotional hunger requires special foods or "comfort foods". Unlike physical hunger, in which any food (even carrots, fruit, a simple piece of bread) can satisfy the impulse, in emotional hunger we are attracted by foods rich in fat or sugar. We feel that we need chocolate or pizza, and nothing else can satisfy us.
- Emotional hunger is associated with "eating unconsciously". Before you know it, you will have finished the bag of chips or the packet of cookies. Most of the time you are inattentive and consequently, the food is not tasted but "thrown in".

- Often, emotional hunger remains even after eating and even when the sense of fullness has been achieved. The stomach says enough but the head pushes us to continue beyond the sense of satiety.
- Emotional hunger is felt in the head. No emptiness or grumbling in the stomach. We think of food, its taste, its smell and we must have it.

EMOTIONAL HUNGER	PHYSICAL HUNGER

Comes on **suddenly**

Uncontrollable or **mindless** eating

Leads to cravings for specific foods, generally **unhealthy and high in calories**

Guilt

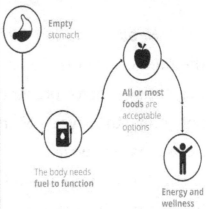

Empty stomach

All or most **foods** are acceptable options

The body needs fuel to function

Energy and wellness

Below are situations commonly related to emotional eating

Habits acquired in childhood - Returning to the memories of the past, it is possible to recover the eating habits present in the family, to trace not only the type of food followed but also situations in which the food, and also some particular food, was used as a reward for certain behaviors (the cake prepared by the mother to cheer us up or a particular dish that was used as a reward).

Social or environmental conditions - There is food everywhere, of all kinds, too! Dozens of television broadcasts are dedicated to this. How can we not be conditioned?
Particular attention must be paid to all those situations in which we experience negative emotions.

Stress - Do you get hungry every time you feel stressed?

It's not just a mental fact. When stress becomes chronic, levels of a hormone called cortisol are raised.

Cortisol "guides" us towards very caloric food choices (very sweet and/or very fatty) because the high presence of this substance "communicates" to our brain that we are preparing for overwork.

Negative emotions - Eating can, temporarily, "silence" emotions such as anger, sadness, anxiety, loneliness. Why? Anxiety causes stomach contractions that can be mistaken for hunger.

Anger causes many muscle groups to contract, including the jaw groups. Eating "crisp" food helps to decongest that part of the muscles that remains stiff. And what about sadness? Without necessarily talking about depression, this is often associated with the lowering of serotonin, a cerebral neurotransmitter whose presence is fundamental. When it goes down we feel depressed and we need to ingest sweet foods that quickly increase the levels of serotonin in our bodies.

Feelings of boredom and emptiness - Boredom can lead to the search for new stimuli and, in this case, we use the sense of taste. If, on the other hand, we experience feelings of emptiness, the simplest and most automatic way to avoid this feeling is to "fill" our stomach.

Most of the time what hinders the adherence to an adequate diet, is dissatisfaction in emotional and social relationships.

Feeling satisfied in family relationships, affection, friendship helps to reduce stress and the presence of negative feelings. The boom in social networks that we are witnessing is the answer to a need for communication, someone to talk to, 24 hours a day.

3. OBESITY

Definition and characteristics of obesity

Obesity is defined as a chronic condition characterized by excessive body weight, through the accumulation of adipose tissue, to such an extent as to adversely affect the state of health.

It is a condition with high prevalence and multifactorial etiology, accompanied by an increased risk of morbidity and mortality and is a consequence of a chronically positive energy balance.

The factors that influence the regulation of the energy balance are many and all connected with the hypothalamus: emotional factors (conviviality, mood, anxiety), gastrointestinal system (gastrointestinal hormones), adipose tissue (adipocytokines), blood circulation (glucose, amino acids), sensitive afferents (sight, taste, smell), cognitive influences (experience, learning), hormones (gonads, surrene, thyroid).

In maintaining the energy balance and its deviations, in addition to the influence of biochemical signals starting from the Central Nervous System, the adipose tissue and the gastroenteric apparatus contribute behavioral influences. In recent years, eating disorders have shown a marked increase in their prevalence. Obesity is divided into essential (95%) linked to genetic and environmental factors and secondary (5%) that can result from endocrine diseases, neurological, genetic forms, drugs, or mental disorders.

Obesity is also divided into android (apple), which prefers men and in which there is an accumulation of adipose tissue mainly at the level of the abdominal area, and ginoid (pear), which is associated with the female sex and is characterized by an accumulation of adipose tissue at the level of thighs, hips and buttocks. (fig. 1)

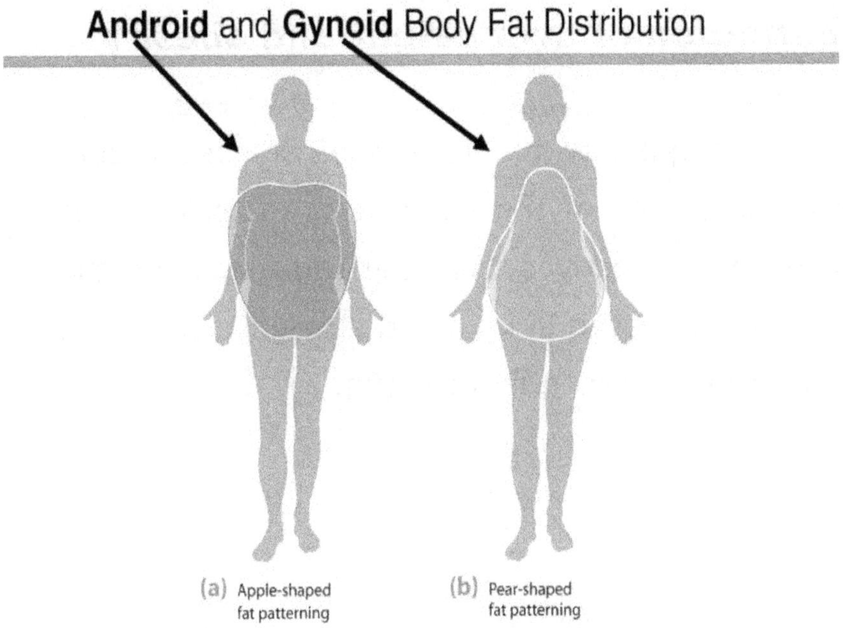

Android and Gynoid Body Fat Distribution

(a) Apple-shaped
fat patterning

(b) Pear-shaped
fat patterning

Fig. 1 *Android and gynoid obesity*

International criteria for the definition of overweight and obesity

To quantify the excess of adipose tissue, the calculation of the body mass index (BMI) is used, which derives from the ratio between the weight expressed in kg and the height per square meter expressed in meters. (fig. 2)

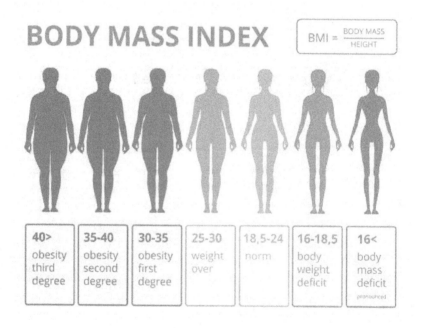

Fig. 2 *Body mass index (BMI)*

However, this index does not differentiate the fat mass from the lean mass (muscle and bone) and does not take into account the distribution of adipose tissue. In this regard, it is important to note that the different comorbidities associated with obesity depend in part on the excess of fat mass and to a large extent on its location.

The adipose tissue that accumulates at the abdominal level would, therefore, represent a marker of the relative inability of the subcutaneous adipose tissue to properly store the excess energy. The accumulation of fat in the ectopic site has metabolically unfavorable effects and increases the expression of cardiovascular risk factors. On the contrary, when the excess energy is stored mainly at the level of the subcutaneous adipose tissue, even in the presence of a chronically positive energy balance, the individual would be protected from the development of diabetes mellitus and cardiovascular diseases.

BMI is a rough estimate of the excess weight, which does not take into account the distribution of fat tissue and whose calculation is influenced by both fat and lean mass. It follows that even modest increases in BMI, where determined exclusively by an increase in visceral adiposity, are associated with an increase in the risk of cardiovascular events and/or mortality, while values even considerably increased in BMI, if linked to an increase in muscle mass, are not necessarily accompanied by an increase in risk. Therefore, the estimate of excess weight identified by the body mass index must be supplemented by the evaluation of the distribution of adipose tissue.

At present, it is possible to use various instrumental examinations that allow estimating with precision the distribution of adipose tissue (ultrasound, CT, MRI). However, it is not possible to use such methods on a large scale, and therefore it is necessary to identify less expensive and simpler methods. In common clinical practice, using a simple tape measure, it is possible to measure some anthropometric parameters such as waist circumference, hip circumference, and the relative ratio. Although this method is well standardized, its reproducibility indeed has some limitations, particularly in large obesity. The waist circumference is a measure adopted by both the National Cholesterol Education Program Adult Treatment Panel III (ATP III) and the International Diabetes Federation (IDF) to define the metabolic syndrome whose exact role in identifying the risk of cardiovascular events remains controversial.

Epidemiology

Obesity is now called a real pandemic, so much so that according to the World Health Organization it is "one of the biggest public health problems of our time". It is estimated that about 300 million obese people live in the world and the seriousness of the problem is destined to worsen both in industrialized countries (North America and Europe) and in developing countries (China, India, South America), with important consequences in terms of economic and health policy. The transfer of Western eating habits from rich countries to poor ones determines an increase in the prevalence of obesity in the latter, but with an important difference: while in developing countries the classes at risk of obesity are the economically privileged zones, where wealth and prestige are translated into greater food availability, in rich countries with a widespread abundance of food the most exposed social classes are those with reduced economic and cultural content, less aware of the problems arising from obesity. According to data provided by the WHO, globally in 2008 1.5 billion adults (over 20 years of age) were overweight. Of these, 200 million men and about 300 million women were obese. Obesity and overweight, previously considered problems only in rich countries, are now growing also in low and middle-income countries.

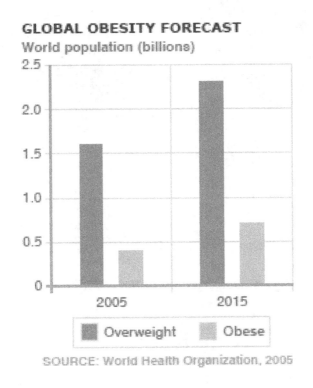

Fig. 3 *Forecast obese and overweight in 2015*

The prevalence of overweight in Ireland and the United Kingdom (England and Scotland) rose rapidly in both sexes by more than 0.8 percentage points per year based on measured data.

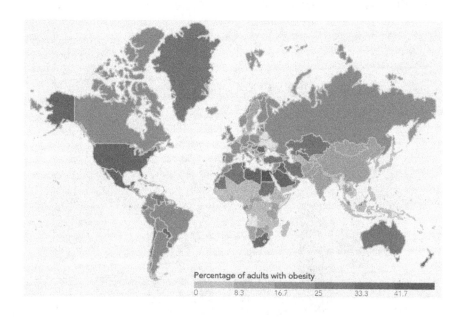

Fig. 4 *Obesity map of the world*

The epidemic is advancing at alarming rates, especially among children. In Switzerland, for example, overweight children increased from 4% in 1960 to 18% in 2003. In England, the United Kingdom, the values increased from 8% to 20% between 1974 and 2003. In various regions of Spain, the prevalence of overweight more than doubled between 1985 and 2002.

Obesity-related complications

Concerning the cardiovascular risk related to obesity there are:
- unchangeable factors: age, sex, genetics
- modifiable factors: increased LDL, decreased HDL, hypertension, diabetes, smoking

As for the cardiometabolic risk, the associated factors are:
- visceral obesity, insulin resistance, atherogenic dyslipidemia, pro-inflammatory state, prothrombotic state

The diseases associated with obesity are numerous:
- cardiovascular: ischaemic heart disease, myocardial infarction, congestive heart failure, sudden death, cerebrovascular accidents, arterial hypertension, left ventricular hypertrophy
- metabolic: dyslipidemia, insulin resistance, NIDDM, hyperuricemia

- gastroenteric: gallstones of the gallbladder, steatosis hepatopathy
- pulmonary: reduction of residual functional capacity, reduction of expiratory reserve volume, reduction of total pulmonary capacity, reduction of maximum expiratory flow, apnea during sleep, obesity hypoventilation syndrome
- arthropathies: gonarthrosis, coxarthrosis, hand arthrosis
- gynecological: polycystic ovary syndrome, alteration of the menstrual cycle, impairment of fertility (from clouding), fetal alterations secondary to maternal obesity
- endocrine: insulin resistance, metabolic syndrome, hyperactivity of the hypothalamus-pituitary-adrenal axis, hypogonadotropic hypogonadism, GH deficiency, polycystic ovary syndrome, hypovitaminosis D
- colorectal and breast cancer

Metabolic and cardiovascular complications: adipose tissue is a real endocrine organ, capable of synthesizing various types of mediators (adipokines, various cytokines, and pro-inflammatory molecules) that act both locally and systemically in the pathogenesis of vascular damage and the development of atherosclerosis.

It is hypothesized that the main alteration underlying the relationship between obesity and cardiovascular risk consists in a state of reduced insulin - sensitivity in various organs and tissues. It is now commonly accepted that insulin - resistance - is involved at various levels in the pathogenesis of major cardiovascular risk factors such as diabetes mellitus, hypertension, and dyslipidemia, mainly in individuals with visceral obesity. Other mechanisms involved in various ways in the pathogenesis of the cardiovascular disease of the obese subject are also known:

- the state of systemic inflammation that can represent an important element in the formation and progression of atherosclerotic plaque both directly and as a promoter of insulin resistance.
- endothelial dysfunction, the pathogenesis of which involves both indirect

mechanisms, such as insulin resistance and the resulting risk factors (diabetes mellitus, hypertension, and dyslipidemia), and direct mechanisms such as the altered production of adipokines and pro-inflammatory cytokines, which results in increased oxidative stress and reduced bioavailability of nitric oxide (NO).

- The prothrombotic state and the increase in sympathetic tone that is associated with an increased risk of cardiovascular events mainly in the patient with central obesity.

Obesity, in particular, visceral obesity, facilitates the appearance of the main risk factors (diabetes mellitus, hypertension, and dyslipidemia) that contribute at various levels to the formation and progression of atherosclerotic plaque while lean mass and perhaps even superficial adipose tissue could play a protective role.

Obesity appears to be closely related to diseases of the gastrointestinal system. The main evidence is with the severity of liver steatosis, colon neoplasm, and acute pancreatitis. Recent literature data indicate that obesity also plays a role in other diseases of the gastrointestinal system.

Gastroesophageal reflux disease (GERD), now better defined as "gastroesophageal reflux syndrome", due to the multiplicity of its clinical manifestations, is characterized by the presence of symptoms or evidence of an erosion of the distal esophagus secondary to the passage of gastric content in a retrograde sense. Within the risk factors, some environmental and alimentary conditions have been identified, frequently correctable, able to act directly on the tone of the lower esophageal sphincter. Among the risk factors of MRGE, obesity has recently been introduced and in the literature, there are now numerous studies that confirm the presence of a direct association between these two morbid conditions, even if sometimes the reports are conflicting.

Cholelithiasis is the most frequent disease of the biliary tract: this condition is mostly asymptomatic or paucisymptomatic and both obesity and overweight are the most important risk factors.

The clinical spectrum of liver diseases related to the accumulation of adipose tissue can be summarized as follows:

- Hepatic steatosis: it is a relatively benign, asymptomatic clinical condition, occasionally related to ultrasound and, above all, not only related to alcohol intake but also secondary to HCV hepatitis or drug damage.

- Non-alcoholic steatohepatitis (NASH): is a clinical condition characterized by the development of inflammation and hepatitis secondary to the accumulation of adipose tissue, which may evolve towards more severe clinical forms such as chronic hepatitis and cirrhosis of the liver. This clinical condition is defined as such because it is absolutely unrelated to alcohol intake.

- Non-alcoholic Fatty Liver Disease (NAFLD): it also develops in the absence of alcohol intake and is considered the hepatic manifestation of metabolic syndrome.

Role of adipose tissue in NAFLD/NASH: the presence of central adipose tissue (abdominal) is a crucial factor for the entry of fatty acids into the portal venous stream with the hematopoietic flow.

The presence of obesity justifies an increased absorption of fatty acids and therefore, in turn, can be an important stimulus to the maintenance of hyperinsulinemia and IR. It has been shown that the accumulation of lipids in the liver increases from 22% to 104% for each 1% increase in adipose tissue in the abdomen.

Respiratory complications are determined by both disposition and excess as such. The rigidity of the thoracic cavity induced by the walls thickened by subcutaneous fat and by the reduced excursions of the diaphragm pushed upwards by the intra-abdominal fat masses, leads to a reduction of all static and dynamic respiratory volumes up to situations of hypoventilation with a deficit of O_2 intake and the elimination of CO_2.

Numerous data in the literature show a direct correlation between the presence of obesity and some types of neoplasms, particularly at the level of the gastro-enteric tract. In particular, an effect of BMI and physical activity on the risk of colorectal cancer seems to have been demonstrated. Moreover, obesity represents one of the emerging factors strongly associated with the development of esophageal adenocarcinoma. Chow WH et al. in 1998 showed that patients with the highest quartile BMI had a risk approximately 2 times higher when correlated with those with the lowest quartile BMI.

The incidence of dermatological pathology is not negligible. In fact, due to the altered ratio between body mass and surface and to the insulating action exerted on the subcutaneous thickened panniculus adipose, the heat dispersion is hindered with the need for a greater production of sweat; for this reason, it is deposited inside the large skin folds and, mixing with sebaceous and peeling skin products, it produces an excellent soil for the proliferation of various bacterial species responsible for irritations and skin infections.

Excess weight is a risk factor for the onset or aggravation of chronic venous insufficiency of the lower limbs, both superficial and deep. The lower limb district is the site of water retention and phlebo-lymphological complications much more than is seen in the lean subjects or morphotypes also because the subject is obese because of the poor and incorrect movement does not use the muscle pump.

Last but not least are the bone and joint complications described in detail below.

Musculoskeletal complications: Hip, knee, tibiotarsal and lumbar spine are the most studied districts from a biomechanical point of view and on the more or less close relationships with the obesity factor. These are subjected to excessive load during common activities to cause damage.

The modalities can be explained by an increase in the force acting on a given surface and thus exerting greater pressure on a given district. This local compressive effect is generally damped and distributed by the affected joint with a consequent limitation of normal joint movements to try to achieve adequate joint relief. However, the chronic consequence of this is the execution of limited and not always correct movements, such as time to cause pathology of misuse not only for the affected joint but also for others involved in the execution of the movement. To keep the pressure acting on a given surface constantly, a proportional adaptation of the accessory joint structures will also be necessary, so that, as the force increases, the system of dumping the loads will necessarily have to be modified.

Taking into account the biomechanics of the articular segment, the gravity of the process is proportional to the arc of movement within which this anomaly is extrinsic.

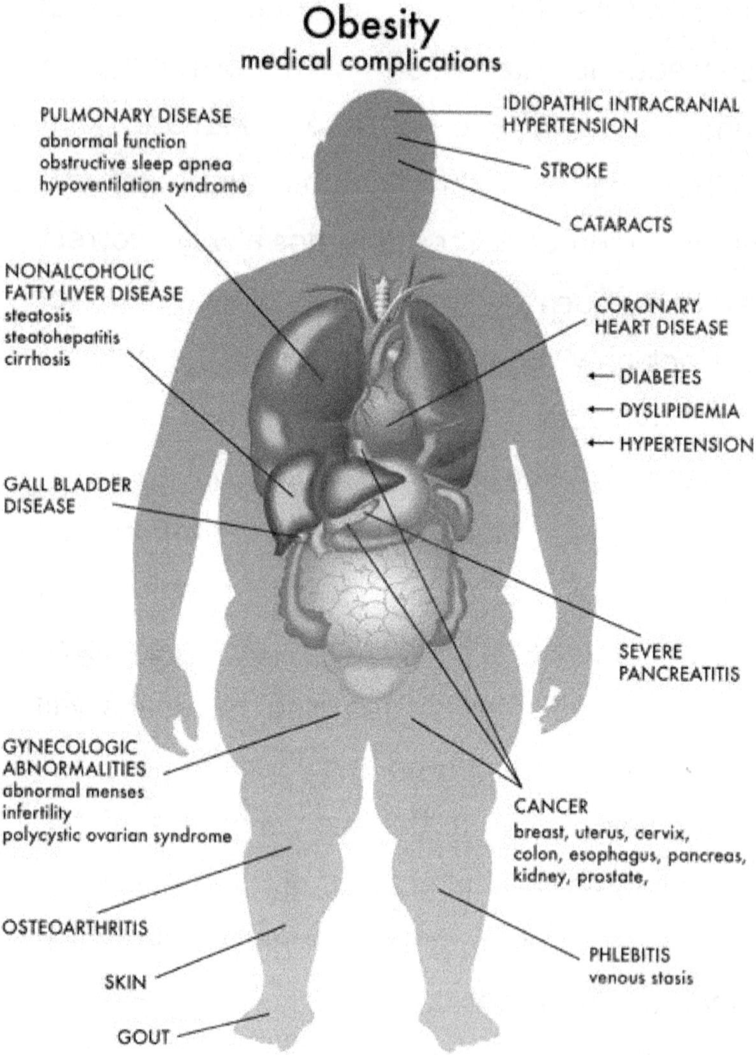

Obesity
medical complications

PULMONARY DISEASE
abnormal function
obstructive sleep apnea
hypoventilation syndrome

IDIOPATHIC INTRACRANIAL
HYPERTENSION

STROKE

CATARACTS

NONALCOHOLIC
FATTY LIVER DISEASE
steatosis
steatohepatitis
cirrhosis

CORONARY
HEART DISEASE

← DIABETES

← DYSLIPIDEMIA

← HYPERTENSION

GALL BLADDER
DISEASE

SEVERE
PANCREATITIS

GYNECOLOGIC
ABNORMALITIES
abnormal menses
infertility
polycystic ovarian syndrome

CANCER
breast, uterus, cervix,
colon, esophagus, pancreas,
kidney, prostate,

OSTEOARTHRITIS

PHLEBITIS
venous stasis

SKIN

GOUT

Fig. 5 *Obesity in medical complications*

One element that characterizes serious obesity, increasingly concerning age is the relative and progressive impoverishment of the muscle share. The condition of sarcopenia has effects both on the metabolic level and on the functional yield. Although it does not represent a disease in the strict sense, it is an important cofactor in the management of inertial loads and the overall motor and ambulatory pattern of the obese patient.

Osteoarticular complications in obesity are frequent, often difficult to separate from the entire clinical picture, with prevalence/incidence rates and criteria for correlating with the obesity factor differing from site to site.

Social costs

The epidemic spread of obesity translates into an enormous social impact since obesity and related diseases lead to a reduction in the quantity and a decline in the quality of life as well as extremely significant direct and indirect health and social costs. The epidemic explosion of obesity, evidence shared by all stakeholders, and certified by the World Health Organization (WHO), has placed the prevention and treatment of obesity among the most important objectives to be achieved in the short term.

What remains to be clarified is represented by the social cost determined by this phenomenon, that is, how much the negative effects of the disease weigh on the living conditions of those who suffer from it, their families and, indirectly, on the whole community, in terms of consumption of economic resources.

A joint study shows data on the prevalence of obesity in the US and Europe. This work, through a systematic review of international studies on the social cost of obesity, has made it possible to estimate the annual social cost of a "generic" obese person at 1.900 USD (1.600 USD of health costs and 300 of non-health costs).

In the United States, around $70 billion a year was spent in the 1990s on medical expenses and the direct and indirect costs of obesity and its complications. In the United States, at least $30 billion has been spent on dietary foods and weight-loss programs. Today in the United States, the cost of obesity to the state is 9% of total medical expenditure, $147 billion.

Associated psychic pathologies

The prevalence data show that obesity represents in most cases the outcome of pathological or otherwise dysfunctional behaviors implemented in the context of a psychological problem, if not a real eating disorder. An eating disorder can be defined as a persistent eating disorder that leads to an alteration in food intake, qualitative and/or quantitative, and that significantly compromises health and psychosocial functioning.

Some dysfunctional eating behaviors are framed as real psychic disorders; other altered modes of feeding can still represent the result of psychological discomfort. Psychiatric disorders related to obesity are represented by Binge Eating Disorder and the Night Eating Syndrome. Among the dysfunctional modes of nutrition are emotional eating and craving.

Obesity, emotional eating, and Craving

Food, sometimes for some individuals can take on an affective or even consolatory value and represents the only possibility of soothing negative emotions often triggered by the stress of daily life.

Food represents a form of self-treatment to alleviate states of melancholy, sadness, anxiety, anger, impotence, insecurity, inadequacy, dissatisfaction.

The term most commonly used to clarify the relationship between food and emotions is that of emotional eating: the tendency to take food to cope better with a set of negative emotions such as anxiety, depression, anger, and loneliness. This construct, however, refers not only to eating habits but also to those feelings that generate in the subject an impulse and desire to take food in response to various emotions.

This behavior, once acquired, tends to repeat itself, triggering a series of vicious circles.

Emotional hunger is therefore caused by emotions, generally negative, and can last for a period of variable length (from a few minutes to a few hours) after the onset of the emotional state. The foods involved are generally 'probity' foods, palatable and rich in fats and carbohydrates.

However, after the outburst of food, negative feelings of guilt and anger towards oneself, related to the feeling of inadequacy and inability to control the impulse to feed, again take over.

Emotional eating has been associated with high levels of depressive symptoms, the consumption of more energy-dense snacks, and a higher body mass.

Episodes of emotional hunger are more common among women and, are related to feelings of low self-esteem, restlessness, anxiety, anger, loneliness, discomfort, and sadness. The act of eating does not derive from a real physiological sensation but is a way of distracting oneself from one's own emotional experiences.

There is a circular relationship between emotions and eating habits: certain emotional experiences can induce the desire for certain foods and these, in turn, can influence, at least in part, the emotional state.

Craving is the intense desire to consume a certain type of food that is difficult to resist. The impulse decreases only when the desired food is consumed. Craving affects the appetite because it can be an incentive to continue eating even when the sense of satiety is sufficient.

Obesity and Binge Eating Disorder

This disorder is characterized by a lack of control over the diet which, in the absence of elimination conduct, leads to various levels of obesity. Finally, the question of how much obesity, in addition to being a possible outcome of an eating disorder, can associate with extreme dietary restrictions, contribute instead to promote its development, is still discussed.

There is a close relationship between obesity and eating disorders if it is true that binge eating leads to various levels of obesity, it is also true that obesity can promote the onset of an eating disorder.

Stunkard first described the subgroup of obese patients who reported recurrent and uncontrolled episodes of binge eating. Many of these subjects could meet the criteria for Binge Eating Disorder (BED) because they show regular binge eating (1-2 episodes over a week for at least 6 months) in the absence of extreme elimination behavior (self-induced vomiting, laxative abuse, diuretics) characteristic of bulimia nervosa. Although the exact prevalence of BED among obese individuals is not known, various data from different obesity research centers agree that 20-30% of obese people treated have binged. The prevalence of BED among obese individuals in the general population is, however, lower, estimated at between 5% and 8%. Nevertheless, since obesity is becoming a statistically relevant problem, this figure cannot be underestimated. Comparing obese individuals with BED to non-BED obese individuals, there are some differences in the clinical and course of events. In particular, binge-eaters have an earlier onset of obesity and the onset of diets and a higher frequency of cyclical weight variations, or the phenomenon defined as "Weight cycling".

Various studies show significant psychopathological differences in the control of eating habits, body image assessment, weight, and self-esteem.

However, uncontrolled eating behavior is not necessarily an artifact of obesity; in fact, it has been shown that obesity present since adolescence can promote the onset of an eating disorder, disorders related to body image and the tendency to low self-esteem and low self-esteem. This would help explain why childhood obesity can increase the risk of eating disorders in adulthood.

A. Recurrent episodes of binge eating

An episode of binge eating is characterized by both of the following:

1. Eating, in a discrete period of time (e.g., within any 2-hour period), an amount of food that is definitely larger than most people would eat in a similar period of time under similar circumstances
2. The sense of lack of control over eating during the episode (e.g., a feeling that one cannot stop eating or control what or how much one is eating)

B. Binge-eating episodes are associated with three (or more) of the following:

1. Eating much more rapidly than normal
2. Eating until feeling uncomfortably full
3. Eating large amounts of food when not feeling physically hungry
4. Eating alone because of being embarrassed by how much one is eating
5. Feeling disgusted with oneself, depressed, or very guilty after overeating

C. Marked distress regarding binge eating is present

D. The binge eating occurs, on average, at least 2 days a week for 6 months

(Note: The method of determining frequency differs from that used for bulimia nervosa; future research should address whether the preferred method of setting a frequency threshold is counting the number of days on which binges occur or counting the number of episodes of binge eating)

E. The binge eating is not associated with the regular use of inappropriate compensatory behavior (e.g., purging, fasting, excessive exercise, etc.) and does not occur exclusively during the course of anorexia nervosa or bulimia nervosa

Tab. 1 *Diagnostic criteria for the Binge Eating Disorder according to DSM-IV-TR*

The role of diet in obese people is controversial: while some studies show the effectiveness of diet in controlling incongruous eating habits, others show that excessive dietary restrictions can undoubtedly be valid causes of an eating disorder. Weight loss is defined as a "necessary but not sufficient" condition for the development of an eating disorder. Empirical studies conducted by the "National Task Force on the prevention and treatment of obesity" do not reinforce the idea that diet induces BED in obese patients undergoing a dietary regime to lose weight.

Obesity and Night Eating Syndrome

Recently, a new entity, called 'Night Eating Syndrome' (NES), has been highlighted which leads to various levels of obesity and which has characteristics that straddle eating disorders and falling asleep disorders. This entity still has no nosological place in the DSM IV and was first described in 1955. Over the years, numerous criteria have been proposed up to the Allison classification (table 2). The picture is characterized by the presence of morning anorexia; evening hyperphagia, insomnia characterized by at least one awakening per night with consumption of snacks during awakening. It also seems very likely that the appearance of Night Eating Syndrome is linked to the presence of stress factors. As far as the incidence is concerned, the data seem to indicate about 2% of the normal-weight population and 9% of obese patients, and 27% of severely obese patients. Evening-night snacks rich in carbohydrates (about 70% of total calories consumed) and in particular the high carbohydrate-protein ratio suggest that night-time feeding is aimed at restoring the disturbed sleep of people with Night Eating Syndrome.

A. The daily pattern of eating demonstrates a significantly increased intake in the evening and/or nighttime, as manifested by one or both of the following:
   1. At least 25% of food intake is consumed after the evening meal
   2. At least two episodes of nocturnal eating per week
B. Awareness and recall of evening and nocturnal eating episodes are present.
C. The clinical picture is characterized by at least three of the following features:
   1. Lack of desire to eat in the morning and/or breakfast is omitted on four or more mornings per week
   2. Presence of a strong urge to eat between dinner and sleep onset and/or during the night
   3. Sleep onset and/or sleep maintenance insomnia are present four or more nights per week
   4. Presence of a belief that one must eat in order to initiate or return to sleep
   5. Mood is frequently depressed and/or mood worsens in the evening
D. The disorder is associated with significant distress and/or impairment in functioning.
E. The disordered pattern of eating has been maintained for at least 3 months.
F. The disorder is not secondary to substance abuse or dependence, medical disorder, medication, or another psychiatric disorder.

Tab. 2 *Night eating syndrome diagnostic criteria*

4. PHYSICAL ACTIVITY AND DYSFUNCTIONAL EATING HABITS

Obesity and physical activity

Lifestyle modification programs recommend physical activity to produce a calorie deficit of at least 400 kcal/day. This can be achieved by educating patients to control their number of steps with a pedometer and then gradually increase the number to reach a value of 10,000-12,000 steps per day, or it can be achieved through jogging (20-40 minutes per day), cycling or swimming (45-60 minutes per day) which can be viable alternatives to walking.

Also, lifestyle changes such as stairs instead of taking the elevator or walking instead of taking the bus can be implemented to maintain weight.

A study of 2013, shows that low levels of cardiovascular fitness and physical activity are related to an increased risk for obesity and metabolic syndrome. The study was carried out on 1610 students at the University of Hampshire between 2010 and 2012; the Mile-Walk Test or Rockport Test and the pedometer were used in the study: The mile walk test consists of a walk test over a distance of one mile, to be walked at the highest possible speed. The variables to consider are time, heart rate after the test, age, gender, and BMI (Body Mass Index). According to the first, three classifications were made: below-average, average or above-average physical performance. Based on the step counter, the classification distinguished severely inactive subjects, those who were not very active, those who were active, and those who were very active.

Stress, physical activity, and nutrition are lifestyle factors that significantly influence the inflammatory profile associated with obesity. Physical activity improves aerobic capacity, strength, muscle growth, body composition, immune function and reduces the risk of developing chronic diseases, cardiovascular diseases, diabetes, and obesity. Active individuals also have a lower incidence of infection than inactive individuals. Other effects of exercise are a decrease in pro-inflammatory cytokines TNF, an increase in anti-inflammatory markers (IL-10), and a decrease in depressive symptoms. Exercise improves immune function and reduces inflammation.

Therefore, exercise is recommended as an effective strategy for positively modifying obesity-related immune function. In conclusion, chronic stress, sedentary behavior, and over-feeding are lifestyle factors conducive to obesity and systemic inflammation.

Non-alcoholic liver steatosis is also often associated with obesity. Even with this disease, exercise seems to be effective as long as it is done regularly and combined with behavioral and dietary changes.

One area of research, which investigates the effect of physical activity on homeostatic mechanisms that control appetite, indicates that active people have better appetite control.

A review by Blundell has shown that, contrary to popular belief that physical activity increases appetite and calorie intake, men and women can tolerate acute energy deficits induced by exercise and not compensate by eating more. Data indicate that this applies to both thin and obese subjects.

Exercise and physical activity can positively influence weight control through self-regulation in eating.

A study in 2013, 72 young people aged 15-19 were evaluated and then divided into 3 groups to evaluate the effects of different types of physical activity: the first group only performed free physical activity, the second only aerobic activity, and the third aerobic activity plus endurance activity. The latter group showed a reduction in leptin levels and better results in body composition than the other 2 groups: this highlights the importance of combining resistance training with aerobic training in the treatment of obesity, as well as nutritional and psychological approaches.

Vitamin D supplementation in overweight and obese adults during endurance training leads to an improvement in the initial peak power, and a high level of vitamin D has been associated with a reduced waist to hip ratio.

Physical activity, Binge Eating, Emotional Eating, and Night Eating Syndrome

Recent literature studies have shown a positive effect of physical activity, in association with cognitive-behavioral therapy, in reducing the weight of individuals with obesity but also in improving depressive symptoms and eating behavior of patients with BED. This improvement was also evident in mild physical activity such as walking. Overall, movement and exercise have been shown to play an important role in the multidisciplinary treatment of Binge Eating Disorder.

This has been further substantiated by other studies. A study carried out on 61 subjects affected by Binge Eating Disorder showed that after cognitive-behavioral therapy there is a significant weight loss, but if we add to the therapy also a nutritional approach and physical activity the weight loss is even more significant. Again, exercise has been shown to improve mood, reduce eating disorders and lead to weight loss.

A further study in 2013 on 211 women aged 25 to 63 showed that aerobic exercise and yoga reduce body mass index by reducing the number of binges typical of the Binge Eating Disorder and it was also seen that exercise combined with cognitive-behavioral therapy is more effective in improving depressive symptoms than therapy alone (CBT).

It has been shown that the risk of developing Binge Eating Disorder related to anxiety sensitivity is significantly reduced in those who practice moderate physical activity and not in those who practice intense physical activity.

A study of 146 severely obese subjects further demonstrated that exercise improves mood, eating behavior, self-regulation and self-efficacy.

A study of 20 adults with Night Eating Syndrome found that after 20 minutes of muscle relaxation exercise there is a significant reduction in stress, anxiety, and immediate post-session salivary cortisol. After practicing the same exercises daily for a week there is a further reduction in stress, anxiety, anger, and depression. These data show that muscle relaxation exercises are an important component in the treatment of Night Eating Syndrome as they reduce the psychological aspects from which it arises.

Another important aspect on which sports activity seems to have an influence is sleep. Alterations in the hypnic pattern are one of the neuro-vegetative symptoms associated with Night Eating Syndrome. Literature data have shown a marked improvement in hypnic activity in subjects subjected to moderate but constant physical activity.

Muscle relaxation techniques are included as effective in the treatment of NES along with pharmacological interventions, cognitive-behavioral therapy, and phototherapy.

Even in forms of obesity characterized by a dysfunctional diet related to negative emotional states, physical activity can be a valuable aid to psychotherapy. This data emerged from a study based on a web questionnaire on the lifestyle of 1562 employees. The topics covered were: sports, emotional eating, alcohol, eating at home and abroad, and smoking.

5. THERAPY

Multidisciplinary approach

Obesity is a complex disease, which requires a complex, multi- and interdisciplinary approach and, possibly, adapted from time to time to the needs of the individual patient. Based on the phenotyping of the patient, a possible path will have to be identified which will involve primary care services in the first place. The next level of intervention will be characterized by a specialized outpatient intervention that will involve the work of a multidisciplinary team consisting of an internist, endocrinologist, nutritionist, psychiatrist, psychologist, dietician, physiotherapist, a graduate in motor sciences.

A multidisciplinary approach can allow the subject to understand the causes of his problem and to put in place in everyday life the behaviors appropriate to achieve the objectives set, modifying progressively dysfunctional behaviors that have contributed to the onset of obesity.

As a chronic condition, obesity can benefit from re-education-rehabilitation programs, such as to encourage a lifestyle change, through the acquisition of appropriate behaviors to achieve the objectives set and their maintenance over time. It is therefore important to set up a program of re-education in the nutritional, behavioral, and motor, where continuous physical activity is considered the primary moment of re-education.

In the hospital environment, it is possible to treat the patient but it is difficult that the experiences of treatment acquired in the hospital are transferred into everyday life. Therefore, in identifying a rehabilitative therapeutic program in a patient suffering from obesity all professional figures will be involved in its implementation.

Somatic and psychopathological comorbidity, disability, reduced overall quality of life in the various phases of the existential cycle are the main components of the clinical evolution of obesity.

Following the biopsychosocial model of the International Classification of Functioning,

Disability and Health (ICF) and using the core set for obese patients, a study group has highlighted the presence of alterations in several specific functional areas [55] on which to intervene with therapeutic rehabilitation programs.

The quality of life questionnaires highlights an important negative effect of obesity not only in the area of physical limitations but also in the more general area of psychological malaise and social functioning. In this regard, it is useful to remember, in addition to the well-known medical complications of obesity, the fact that this condition is very often associated with reduced psychophysical well-being, eating disorders (in particular Binge Eating Disorder, "BED" and Night Eating Syndrome, "NES"), low self-esteem and depression, consequences of severe and insidious social stigma that affects those affected by this disease.

In recent years it has been shown that there is a relationship independent of the presence of chronic diseases between BMI and different degrees of disability in daily activities of life, such as walking or climbing steps, both for body mass and related obesity symptoms (pain, dyspnea, sleep disorders).

It has also been reported that obese people face not only a reduction in life expectancy but also a significant reduction in the number of years without disability (5.7 for men and 5.02 for women). The result is an increase in the number of requests for intervention, above all rehabilitation and social, which accompany the attempts at medical treatment (diet therapy, drugs) and surgical treatment of obese patients.

The literature suggests a hierarchy in the appearance of disabilities in the presence of obesity: the first functions involved are those related to the lower limbs (strength and balance maintenance) because they are more vulnerable than those related to the upper limbs (strength and manual ability).

It should be noted that the prevalence of obesity is increasing significantly even among the elderly (> 65 years): in this age group, the effects on disabilities of obesity and aging end up adding up.

Obesity adds to the physiological impoverishment of lean mass (sarcopenia) in causing disability and even more significantly than when each of the two factors is taken separately.

Finally, the obese subject finds himself in an almost hostile condition from a medical, educational, and occupational point of view, which is related to the degree of obesity. The phenomenon of stigmatization is associated with an increase in the depressive state and a reduction in self-esteem (more evident in women), with the use of primitive, immature, and poorly adaptive defense mechanisms (e.g. removal, denial, projection, and splitting) that involve a greater distortion of reality. Social exclusion and discrimination in employment are part of the stigma.

Being obese or sometimes even simply overweight can be a criterion for exclusion in the context of recruitment or participation in open competitions. In contrast to the disabled, who are considered by society as "not guilty" of their condition and therefore obviously justified and helped, the obese person is held "responsible" and as such are penalized.

The objectives of metabolic-nutritional-psychological rehabilitation in the treatment of obesity (MRI) in the obese person can be summarized as follows:

A. short-term objectives:

1. to add a loss of fat mass that allows an improvement of the risk factors and control of the associated pathologies;
2. optimize residual functional capacities and basic autonomies of daily/social life to reduce present disabilities;
3. correct the patient's attitude towards nutrition and physical activity; treat any clinical eating disorders (e.g. BED, NES);
4. reassess the associated medical and psychiatric pathologies and develop a treatment consistent with the current guidelines and appropriate to the clinical responses of the subject.

B. long-term objectives:

1. maintain a correct lifestyle: adequate nutrition for energy and nutrient supplies to one's own needs with the adoption of a Mediterranean dietary model;
2. regular physical activity of at least 2 hours/week, at medium-low load (50% of maximum heart rate);

3. maintain the fat mass loss achieved over time to control the associated risk factors;
4. maintain the basic autonomy of daily/social life and reduce the present disabilities;
5. maintain a good glycemic compensation, a correct lipidemic and prothydic structure;
6. reduce PA and CF in the presence of altered metabolic parameters and cardiovascular risk;
7. reduce drug therapy for arterial hypertension, diabetes mellitus, dyslipidemia, etc..
8. adjust any psychopharmacological therapies based on therapeutic efficacy and effects on body weight and metabolism (it is known that most psychotropic drugs promote body weight gain and related obesity complications).

Lifestyle changes

Diet

A substantial contribution to the Epidemic of Obesity and Overweight in both Western and developing countries was given by the increase in consumption, both in childhood and adulthood, of foods with high energy density but low nutritional value (foods with visible fat, soft drinks with caloric sweeteners, bakery products/snacks, confectionery), to which must be added the sharp reduction in regular physical exercise during work and leisure time and when moving from home.

The non-pharmacological therapy of obesity and overweight should, therefore, be directed to the correction of incorrect eating habits and the resumption of physical activity compatible with the patient's current clinical conditions: in other words, it is often necessary to establish a physical and nutritional rehabilitation program. This integrated intervention, if appropriate, is not only corrective but enhances the effectiveness of the individual components, is well known the interaction between type of diet and type of muscle exercise practiced and optimizes the use of the necessary drugs for any possible morbid associations.

In the absence of other specific therapeutic indications, the obesity correction intervention must aim at a reduction of about 10% of the initial weight, especially in the case of obesity of grade I or II, or franc overweight, in a reasonable time, from 4 to 6 months. Only in the case of grade III obesity does the need for initial weight reduction exceed this conventional share of 10%.

In essence, it has been possible to observe that the stable loss of 10% of the initial body weight, obtained by a prevalent loss of adipose tissue, is adequate to correct the morbid component due to excessive adiposity. Every dietary intervention, carried out both in the context of public and private institutions, should never leave out a component of simple but complete information and nutrition education. Only in the case of a clear suspicion of eating disorders is there an indication for a clinical-diagnostic intervention of a psychotherapeutic type.

The dietary restriction must be evaluated based on the patient's energy expenditure, preferably measured (resting metabolism measured with indirect calorimetry in standard conditions or calculated using the appropriate predictive formulas [to prefer that of Harris-Benedict or WHO] and multiplied by 1.3). In general, an energy restriction of between 500 and 1000 kcal (2095 and 4190 KJ) compared to the calculated daily energy expenditure is recommended. It is not recommended to prescribe outpatients low-calorie diets with a daily intake of less than 1300 kcal (5447 KJ) per day.

The composition of the Diet must meet the criteria of an adequate ratio between calories of protein origin and calories of non-protein origin: the more the non-protein calories are reduced, the greater must be the protein contribution of the Diet. In general, proteins must be of good biological value and come from both animal and vegetable protein sources: we recommend a contribution of 0,8 - 1 g of protein per kg of desirable weight (only in exceptional cases can a protein intake of 1,3 -1,5 g per kg of desirable weight be achieved). For desirable weight means the weight corresponding to a body mass index of 22,5 kg/m2 calculated for the corresponding height of the patient.

Non-protein calories must come from foods with a low glycemic index as regards the carbohydrate content and from vegetable fats (excluding coconut and palm) mainly for seasoning, preferring extra virgin olive oil. It is not recommended to limit the intake of carbohydrates below 120-130 g/day or to limit fats below 20-25 g/day.

The choice of foods to be prescribed is therefore based on choices of mainly vegetable foods as provided for in the Mediterranean food model: cereals, legumes, vegetables, fruit as regards carbohydrates and a share of dietary proteins, preferably extra virgin olive oil for fats for seasoning, lean meat and fish (at least 2-3 times a week) for animal protein sources. A regular intake of milk, yogurt, and some other "low-fat" milk derivatives should be guaranteed to complete the protein intake and especially the calcium intake.

With regard to the distribution of meals during the day, it seems appropriate to encourage the practice of a relatively abundant breakfast (semi-skimmed milk, cereals, fruit, yogurt) and a "light" dinner to be consumed in the early hours of the evening. The practice of snacks, especially mid-morning and afternoon, has no specific indications for the correction of obesity but should be considered in terms of metabolic problems of the patient or specific individual preferences.

Therapeutic education

Therapeutic Education means the continuous therapeutic action characterized by "accompanying" the patient, "getting together" in the path of chronic disease, aimed at negotiating and agreeing on the implementation of possible interventions aimed at achieving the maximum clinical result and the best-perceived quality of life for each patient.

Therapeutic education, according to the definition of the WHO 1998, should allow the patient to acquire and maintain the skills that allow him to achieve optimal management of their lives with the disease. Its importance was first recognized in 1972 thanks to the work of L. Miller and became a continuous process integrated into health care. Therapeutic education is an indispensable moment in the management of chronic patients. Its purpose is to implement knowledge about the disease and its management and to modify behaviors related to it to achieve better management of the same; moreover, education allows to grasp and manage the psychological aspects related to the disease itself and therefore, in addition to the role of information on the practical management of the disease, education aims to contribute to improving the quality of life.

Behavioral therapy techniques associated with lifestyle changes are more effective in treating obese patients than lifestyle intervention alone. Therapeutic education in the short to the medium-term treatment of obesity is more effective if planned and organized for small groups of patients. The therapeutic education of obesity must be guaranteed, within the team, by the different professional figures (doctor, nurse, dietitian, social and health educator, psychiatrist, psychologist, graduate in motor sciences) specifically qualified based on continuous professional training in the educational activity. Motivation is fundamental to obtain therapeutic adherence and stable weight loss. The motivation for change and the use of therapeutic education take into account above all conscious mental processes and cannot address those less probable unconscious aspects that support the most tenacious resistance. Given these premises, the main techniques, also derived from cognitive-behavioral therapy, which are the cornerstones of therapeutic education, are:

1. The therapeutic alliance
2. Therapeutic compliance
3. Motivation
4. Problem-solving
5. Empowerment
6. Narrative medicine

Therapeutic alliance

Continuous care for the chronically ill must be considered from a temporal perspective since it must be the subject of a therapeutic contract. A contract in which both parties agree to respect several elements. Since this is a therapy, it implies careful management of the objectives to be negotiated with the patient. This sort of pact or therapeutic alliance has amply demonstrated its effectiveness in the field of chronic disease management. In a therapeutic alliance based on the trust and support of the caregivers, the patient will be able to regain motivation and accept the change in lifestyle and treatment needs. The continuous assistance of the chronically ill cannot be subject to the prescription of pre-established rules provided by the health care staff to all patients: the patient suffering from chronic pathology is not a passive vessel of the therapy, but the real protagonist of the therapeutic act.

Therapeutic compliance

The achievement of therapeutic objectives in the management of the chronic disease requires the acquisition of appropriate behaviors related to lifestyle and drug therapy, the patient can behave most advantageously only if he can take on complex management skills, which can not be transmitted only by the act of prescription. Medicine has borrowed the term "compliance" from physics. This term is used in medicine to indicate the patient's adherence to the therapeutic prescriptions. The transposition of the notion of compliance in the field of the doctor-patient relationship can generate problems: the patient cannot be compared to an elastic object, more or less resistant to the action exerted by the health care personnel and so the therapeutic relationship between doctor and patient is configured as an act of force. The patient's decision cannot depend on external pressure, warnings, or persuasion. For these reasons, the term therapeutic compliance is currently replaced by therapeutic adherence, which better underlines the need for active patient involvement in therapeutic decisions.

Motivation

The meaning of motivation can be variously indicated which:
- needs, beliefs that determine a certain character
- the urge to complete an action
- the tendency to devote energies to achieve a goal
- feelings that push an individual towards a particular object

The term motivation comes from the Latin MOTUS, which means "push of a subject in the direction of an object". This etymological origin well expresses the value of the motivation for the attainment of a stable lifestyle change, the ultimate goal of therapeutic education.

In particular, what conditions a real push for stable change is the presence of what is called motivational-readiness. This concept implies the existence of a real push towards the objective and of a concomitant condition of readiness, i.e.

current and effective willingness to undertake the therapeutic path. A person can believe that he or she is motivated, without being motivated. In this case, the conflicts that are present in the initial condition (for example, the state of obesity), prevent the patient to move easily from that condition.

A subject may also be motivated, but not ready because there are serious obstacles that prevent him from facing the problem.

The motivation for change can go through several phases even more times before the patient reaches a stable change. The phases of change are represented by meditation (the subject is aware of the problem, sometimes accepts the change, sometimes rejects it), determination (a phase limited in time in which the decision to change may appear), action (the change begins, but the path is dotted with steps backward), maintenance (with an active work of consolidation and prevention of relapses) and finally the relapse (if you do not have the permanent exit from the problem, may appear a relapse that starts a new process).

The motivation to change must, therefore, pre-exist in the patient as a substratum of the therapeutic path, but at the same time, the clinician has the task of shaping it and directing it to the proposed educational project, to ensure the therapeutic alliance with the patient. It is equally important that the clinician knows how to strengthen the readiness-motivational in the patient during the different phases of the path, to improve the adherence of the same to the care project and the implementation of the latter.

Problem-solving

Problem Solving is one of the tools of therapeutic education that allows the patient to equip himself with the necessary skills to manage his behavior. Learning to cope with and autonomously manage external stimuli, as well as personal thoughts and emotions, is of fundamental importance during the therapeutic process of weight loss. The eating behavior and sedentary attitude of obese patients are often strongly marked by psychological elements, both contingent, and stable (of personality).

Problem-solving is, therefore, a methodology of objective self-analysis that the patient can implement concerning their attitudes towards food and their tendency to lose control. From the application of such a methodology, the patient can acquire the capacity of self-observation and self-criticism to recognize and face situations at risk, thus learning to manage their eating behavior and their lifestyle in general. The problem-solving technique is divided into a series of phases, first provides for the recognition of the situation at risk or obstacle (the phase of recognition of the "problem"), then provides for the search for possible strategies and alternatives to be implemented to overcome it. Once the patient has learned to recognize the obstacle, he will be able to choose the most appropriate and feasible solution to overcome it and remain faithful to his path of care. The strategies that the clinician can propose, or that the patient himself can hypothesize to manage in an alternative way the situation at risk (loss of control over food, rather than giving up physical activity), are various, so the patient must learn to identify the most suitable situation for himself and then experiment with the regular implementation.

Empowerment

The literal definition of empowerment is "empowerment" or rather the set of knowledge, relational skills, and competencies that allow an individual or a group to set goals and develop strategies to achieve them using existing resources. Empowerment is a process of social action through which individuals, organizations, and communities acquire competence over their lives to change their social and political environment to improve equity and quality of life.

As a result, empowerment is both a concept and a process for achieving goals. There are two main elements of empowerment: the feeling of being able to perform effective actions to achieve a goal and the ability to perceive the influence of their actions on events. In this sense, the importance of seeking a sense of self-esteem and self-efficacy with which the individual will be driven to "learn to do" and then "to do" emerges. The patient becomes aware of being effective in changing the events of his or her life, of implementing self-esteem, and of interpreting failures also like moments of learning. Through these assumptions also changes the role of the caregiver who becomes a figure to accompany the patient, to share decisions, stimulate autonomy and a sense of responsibility, identify needs, and promote personal growth.

Narrative medicine

Narrative medicine uses autobiography as a tool through which a patient suffering from a chronic disease can find new strategies and energies to face his life. The aim is to have the patient write a biography of his or her illness to stimulate him or her to deal with himself or herself and with his or her illness. A greater awareness of one's history modifies how the patient sees the present and future, giving new ideas and new keys to interpretation.

Moreover, this tool stimulates self-care and empowers the patient by strengthening existing resources. In everyday life we use our narrative skills to tell others, to say something about ourselves, about our past, but also about our future expectations. In the same way, the patient tells the doctor his own "story of illness", and this is probably a true and complete description of his illness.

Life is not the one we have lived but the one we remember and how we remember it to tell it. Narrative medicine, which among its founders has two Harvard psychiatrists, Kleinman and Good, therefore deserves the attention it has received in recent times. Today, in an era in which medicine has reached extraordinary goals of technological development and the concept of evidence-based medicine is now very familiar, we felt the need to recover the doctor-patient relationship, where the narrative of the patient's pathology to the doctor is considered equal to the signs and clinical symptoms of the disease itself. This Narrative Based Medicine (NBM) refers not only to the patient's experience but also to the experiences of the doctor-patient relationship.

Treatment

Pharmacological therapy

In the last 25 years, more than 120 drugs have been studied for the treatment of obesity. Only one drug in the United States and Italy, Orlistat, is still approved for long-term therapy. The other drugs studied for long-term treatment, Sibutramine and Rimonabant, have been suspended from the market for safety reasons (EMA/808179/2009, EMA/H/A-107/1256 of 21/01/2010).

General indications for drug therapy and the start of therapy: in Italy, the pharmacological treatment is reserved only for adults, while in the USA there is an indication for the treatment of subjects over 12 years of age, with Orlistat.

Adults

Pharmacological treatment should only be considered after the effectiveness of diet, exercise, and, where indicated, cognitive-behavioral therapy has been assessed and these therapeutic approaches are ineffective either in inducing weight loss or in maintaining lost weight.

The decision to start treatment and drug choice (when possible) should be made after discussion with the patient, both of the potential benefits and limitations of the drug, including its mechanism of action, side effects, and potential impact on the patient's motivation. When prescribing drug treatment, the practitioner should provide information, support, and counseling on diet, physical activity, and behavioral strategies to be adopted.

Children

Pharmacological treatment is not generally recommended for children under 12 years of age. As already mentioned, in the USA, unlike Italy, the use of Orlistat is authorized in subjects over the age of 12 years.

Sibutramine was suspended in Europe by the EMA in January 2010, based on data from the SCOUT study that showed the appearance of a greater number of non-fatal cardiovascular and cerebrovascular events in patients with a history of cardiovascular disease and diabetes and, therefore, where the drug was in itself contraindicated.

Continuation of therapy and discontinuation of the drug

Pharmacological treatment may be indicated to maintain weight loss, rather than to induce further weight loss. This is where the concept of cyclic or intermittent therapy comes in.

Where there are concerns about adequate micronutrient intake, consideration should be given to supplementing the patient with vitamins and minerals, particularly for the most vulnerable patient groups, such as the elderly (who are themselves at risk of malnutrition) and young people (who need vitamins and minerals for growth and development).

Regular treatment monitoring is recommended to monitor the effect of the drug and to strengthen nutritional advice and adherence to proper lifestyles.

Suspension of drug treatment should be considered in patients who do not lose weight.

The rate of weight loss may be slower in patients with type 2 diabetes.

Therefore, the objectives of therapy may be less rigid in these patients than in non-diabetic patients. These goals should be agreed upon with the patient and reviewed regularly. Patients whose medication is discontinued should be adequately supported in maintaining their lost weight.

Orlistat

Orlistat should be administered only as one of several approaches in a comprehensive treatment plan aimed at treating obesity in adult patients who meet the following criteria:

- a BMI of 28.0 kg/m2 or more with associated risk factors
- a BMI of 30,0 kg/m2 or more.

Therapy should only be continued beyond 3 months if the patient has lost at least 5 % weight since the start of drug therapy.

The decision to use the drug for more than 12 months (usually for weight maintenance) should be made after careful discussion with the patient about the potential benefits and limitations of treatment.

In general, it is believed that the effectiveness of anti-obesity drugs is modest, with a weight loss of less than 5 kg minus the placebo effect after 1 year of treatment, both with Orlistat and with Rimonabant and Sibutramine. This modest figure is however relevant because the use of a drug significantly increases the number of patients who manage to achieve a decrease of more than 5-10% compared to the initial weight one year after the start of therapy.

The suspension of pharmacotherapy, as well as the suspension of other therapeutic interventions, is accompanied by a recovery of lost weight.

Combined therapy with two drugs (Orlistat and Sibutramine) is not superior to therapy with a single drug. Nevertheless, the combination of two active ingredients is the basis of new drugs at an advanced stage of the study.

It should always be stressed that the pharmacological approach should not be understood so much as an approach capable in itself of reducing body weight, but rather a tool that allows you to manage weight and, therefore, to facilitate its maintenance over time. Also, drug therapy can improve the metabolic profile of obese patients with complications.

Last but not least, the role of drugs in the treatment of obesity should also be understood as an aid in encouraging the patient to adhere to the global therapeutic approach, which also includes nutritional treatment, lifestyle change, and cognitive-behavioral therapy.

Pharmacological therapy should be considered in individuals with a BMI $\geq$ 30 kg/m2 not responding to diet and exercise, or a BMI > 27 kg/m2 for those with obesity-related diseases.

Once an anti-obesity drug is prescribed, patients should be actively engaged in a lifestyle change program that provides the strategies and tools necessary to achieve significant weight loss and to keep the weight as constant as possible over time.

Bariatric Surgery

Bariatric surgery should be considered as a therapeutic option in adult patients (age 18-60 years) with severe obesity (BMI> 40 kg/m2 or BMI>35 kg/m2 if with associated comorbidity) where previous attempts to lose weight and/or maintain weight loss with non-surgical techniques have failed and where there is a willingness for prolonged postoperative follow-up.

Bariatric surgery is considered contraindicated in patients with one of the following conditions: the absence of verifiable medical treatment, inability to participate in a prolonged follow-up protocol, major psychiatric disease, alcoholism, and drug addiction, reduced life expectancy, inability to care for themselves in the absence of adequate family and social support.

Bariatric surgery may be considered as a therapeutic option in adolescent patients with BMI>35 kg/m2 in the presence of severe comorbidities (type 2 diabetes mellitus, moderate to severe obstructive apnea syndrome, severe steatohepatitis) or with BMI>40 kg/m2 in the presence of other comorbidities.

Also, all of the following criteria must be met: Tanner IV or V stage; skeletal maturity at least 95% completed; ability to understand which changes in diet and physical activity will be necessary for the optimal postoperative outcome; adequate maturity of judgment, with an appropriate understanding of the benefits and potential risks of surgery; adequate social support without evidence of abuse or neglect; adequate therapy of possible psychiatric comorbidity; demonstration that the family and the patient have the ability and motivation to adhere to pre- and post-operative prescriptions.

Bariatric surgery can be considered as a therapeutic option in patients over 60 years of age with severe obesity only after a careful individual assessment of the risks and benefits, of the potential improvement in the quality of life and mortality risk in the short to medium term. In elderly patients, the primary objective is to improve the quality of life and functional autonomy.

There is currently insufficient evidence to recommend in general terms the application of bariatric surgery in patients with BMI lower than the threshold of indication considered by the current guidelines.

The possibility remains open that this therapeutic option may be effective in terms of risk-benefit ratio in patients with BMI 30/35 kg/m2 and severe comorbidity not sufficiently controlled by optimal medical therapy, with particular reference to diabetic patients. In any case, this hypothesis should only be explored in the context of long-term controlled studies.

Bariatric surgery must be performed in dedicated facilities that have the necessary skills and requirements: dedicated multidisciplinary team, medical and paramedical staff with specific cultural and technical skills, clinical diagnostic and selection of patients according to criteria of appropriateness, minimum guaranteed operating program, adequate technical equipment for the care of patients with severe obesity, adequate post-operative care, ability to manage early and late complications.

The preoperative evaluation of the bariatric candidate, in addition to the standard evaluation required for any type of surgery, must investigate the following additional areas: endocrinological, dialectological, cardiovascular, respiratory, gastroenterological, psychological-psychiatric, dietary-nutritional.

The reduction of operating risks can be maximized by optimizing the control of complications and the implementation of appropriate thrombo-embolic prophylaxis and antibiotics.

The following surgical procedures are currently supported by literature data including sufficiently large cases and with an adequately prolonged follow-up:

1. Interventions that limit the introduction of food:

1.1 predominantly mechanical (restrictive interventions):

- an adjustable gastric bandage;
- vertical gastroplasty;
- sleeve gastrectomy;

1.2 with mainly functional action:

- gastric bypass and variants.

2. Interventions that limit the absorption of energy:

- biliopancreatic diversion according to Scopinaro
- duodenal switch.

The laparoscopic approach should be considered the first choice in bariatric surgery as it is advantageous compared to the open one in terms of better postoperative course and reduction of complications.

At the moment, we do not have evidence-based data that would allow us to initiate each patient into a particular bariatric procedure. Factors that may be useful for the choice of intervention are related to the patient (age; sex; overweight and fat distribution; body composition and energy consumption; complications and morbid conditions associated with particular reference to type 2 diabetes; eligibility and quality of life; socio-economic and cultural level; motivation and collaborative capacity; family and environmental support and geographical distance from the place of care), to the method (technical execution; results; specific complications, immediate and late) and the surgeon (technical ability; culture and experience, generic and specific; structure and health system).

An appropriate follow-up path should be offered, ideally and possibly for life, to all patients operated on by the interdisciplinary team of the reference bariatric surgery center. The follow-up should include the diagnosis and treatment of all events, not necessarily surgical, in the short and long term, specifically related to the intervention, as well as the management of comorbidities and complications.

6. EFFECTIVENESS OF PHYSICAL ACTIVITY

Effects of physical activity

Sedentariness is now identified as the fourth risk factor for mortality, responsible for 6% of deaths globally, after arterial hypertension (responsible for 13%), tobacco use (9%), and hyperglycemia (6%). Overweight and obesity are responsible for 5% of global mortality.

Today, physical inactivity is estimated to be the main cause of about 21-25% of breast and colon cancers, 27% of cases of diabetes, and about 30% of cases of ischaemic heart disease.

Low levels of physical activity have important repercussions on the general health of populations, with a significant increase in the prevalence of non-communicable diseases (cardiovascular diseases, diabetes, and cancer) and their risk factors (arterial hypertension, hyperglycemia, and overweight).

This is particularly relevant when one considers that about half of the disease burden in adulthood is currently attributable to non-communicable diseases, both in developing and industrialized countries.

The practice of physical activity and health status are closely related, in all age groups. The rich literature shows that people with higher levels of physical activity have a reduced incidence of mortality from all causes, ischaemic heart disease, hypertension, cerebral vasculopathy, diabetes mellitus, metabolic syndrome, colon and breast cancer, and depression. They also have a more favorable body composition and biochemical profile in terms of cardiovascular prevention, diabetes and bone diseases (osteoporosis and fractures), and better cardiorespiratory capacity.

Cardiorespiratory fitness (CRF) is defined as the ability of the circulatory, respiratory, and muscular systems to supply oxygen during sustained physical activity. Normally CRF is expressed as maximum oxygen uptake (VO2 max) or MET (metabolic equivalents, 1 MET = 3,5 ml/kg- 1·min-1 of O2), evaluated by a maximum stress test on a treadmill or cycle ergometer. The CRF is not only a reliable measure of regular physical activity but also an important indicator of people's health. Cardiorespiratory fitness is associated with cardiovascular morbidity and mortality in both men and women, independently of other risk factors. A moderate or high level of CRF reduces the risk of mortality from all causes in both sexes and the protective effect is independent of age, ethnicity, adiposity, smoking, alcohol, and health status

The dose-response analysis published in the 2009 meta-analysis, which included 33 studies with a total of 102980 participants, shows that the increase of only one CRF MET is associated with a 13% reduction in mortality from all causes and a 15% reduction in the risk of cardiovascular events. In favor of the CRF as an important mortality risk factor, there are two prospective studies in which the effect of the change in CRF overtime on mortality from all causes was examined. Both studies, performed in male subjects, show that the improvement or worsening of CRF during an average follow-up of 5 or 7 years is associated with a reduction or increase in the risk of death from all causes.

These data indicate the importance of assessing the cardiorespiratory fitness of patients at cardiovascular risk and of improving their CRF through training programs. A low CRF conferring a high risk of cardiovascular events for the age group of 40 years is 9 MET for men and 7 MET for women, at 50 years is 8 and 6 MET and at 60 years 7 and 5 MET, respectively.

Anaerobic physical activity program in sedentary individuals already after 3-6 months can improve CRF by 1-3 METs and substantially reduce cardiovascular risk or mortality from all causes.

Although this issue is still under discussion, the favorable effects of physical activity seem to be independent of those on weight loss.

A study evaluating mortality about obesity and fitness showed that low physical capacity, and therefore a lower level of habitual physical activity, was an independent predictor of mortality for all causes, even after correction for adiposity and that obese people who had good physical capacity had a lower mortality rate than normal-weight but physically inactive.

Because of its favorable effects on global health, regular physical activity is also recommended in individuals with obesity or overweight, regardless of its effect on weight, as an important preventive and therapeutic tool, by all public health agencies and scientific organizations, such as the National Heart, Lung and Blood Institute, the Centers for Disease Control in the United States, and various medical societies such as the American College of Sports Medicine and the American Heart Association, the American Medical Association, the American Academy of Family Physicians.

The recommendations are quite consistent. In an adult person, at least 150 minutes of moderate aerobic activity per week is recommended, or at least 75 minutes of vigorous aerobic activity or an equivalent combination of moderate and vigorous aerobic activity. Aerobic activity may be performed in periods of at least 10 minutes.

For additional health benefits, an adult may increase moderate aerobic physical activity to 300 minutes per week, or 150 minutes of vigorous aerobic physical activity, or an equivalent combination of moderate and vigorous aerobic physical activity.

There is limited evidence of the effectiveness of an activity against resistance in promoting the increase or maintenance of lean mass and loss of fat mass during a low-calorie diet. However, there is evidence of its ability to favorably modify certain cardiovascular risk factors (HDL cholesterol, LDL cholesterol, insulinemia, blood pressure). Strength activities, involving major muscle groups, should be undertaken at least two days a week. Maintaining good muscle strength reduces the risk of injury with aerobic activity.

Exercise and prevention of obesity

The nosological entity overweight/obesity is certainly a multifactorial pathology, that is defined by complex interactions between genetic, hormonal, and social and environmental factors (incorrect dietary habits and sedentary lifestyle).

Numerous studies support the strong scientific evidence of the protective role played by an active lifestyle towards weight gain/obesity and of the favorable role played by a sedentary lifestyle. Over the last few decades, thanks to the process of industrialization, the performance of physically active jobs and professions have been drastically reduced, energy consumption for transport has been reduced (cars, lifts), while leisure time dedicated to practices not physically active (TV, computers) has increased. Therefore, the modern lifestyle in developed countries, characterized by low daily energy expenditure and abundant food availability, frequently produces a positive energy balance with a continuous increase in the prevalence of obesity, which has become a public health problem with an epidemic spread.

About the prevention of weight gain, it should be remembered that the primary prevention of obesity begins with maintenance and not weight loss. The risk of weight gain varies over time and so does the need for physical activity to prevent this from happening. To date, no scientific studies are validating this concept, but there is cross-type evidence on the existence of an inverse relationship between weight status (body weight or BMI, Body Mass Index m2/kg) and physical activity and it is clear a (minimum) dose-response relationship between weight loss (or BMI) and increased levels of physical activity. Many studies support the need to perform at least 150 mins of physical activity per week to control long-term body weight.

In a 12-month randomized controlled study, which aimed to achieve 300 minutes of moderate physical activity per week, was found further evidence on the effectiveness of increased physical effort in preventing weight gain. These 3 studies together support the evidence that the practice of 150- 250 min per week of moderate physical activity, with an energy equivalent of 1200-2000 kcal (50000-8500 KJ, about 18-30 km per week), is sufficient to prevent a weight gain (> 3% of weight) in most adults.

The evaluation of several well-conducted studies, therefore, highlights the importance of achieving the goal of at least 150 minutes per week of aerobic activity, of moderate intensity, spread over several days, with sessions lasting at least 10 minutes (for example 30 minutes per day for 5 days) and without exceeding volumes of 300 minutes per week of activity, the threshold above which the benefit decreases and increases the risk of musculoskeletal injury.

Alternatively, 75 minutes per week of vigorous aerobic physical activity or an equivalent combination of moderate and vigorous activity may be practiced. Two days a week, strength activities can be practiced, involving the major muscle groups.

The rehabilitation program of the obese subject

Criteria for the choice of physical activity

When choosing a physical activity, the degree of effectiveness of the physical activity in fat reduction, the practicability (about the clinical picture) and the fun must be taken into account. The weight loss is greater the muscle mass involved, for example in activities such as running, swimming, and gymnastics. It should be borne in mind that there are physical and psychological limitations for the obese in some "land" sports such as running, football, etc..

Especially in the first periods of activity, obesity is a limit to the efficiency of performance, and therefore involves psychological damage and an excessively heavy strain on the joints, especially the lower limbs. There are sports such as swimming and cycling that are always recommended because they involve a great deal of energy but not a great deal of joint stress. The training gradually increases the physical efficiency of the individual, gradually disappears the physical limits to performance. Bodyweight decreases and improves body composition (lean mass to fat ratio), increase strength, endurance, and improves motor skills. All this leads to the breaking down of psychological limits, often a brake on obese subjects, there is a growth in self-esteem and self-confidence.

To reinforce these results, in addition to the improved ability to perform, also contributes to the better physical appearance obtained through exercise and proper nutrition. Therefore, making an obese patient able to correctly carry out a continuous program of physical activity, as well as allowing him a more active lifestyle in everyday life, leads to a certain improvement in the quality of life and self-esteem, and this is only partly related to weight loss.

Ways and timing

All patients with excess weight should try to exercise continuously. Combining physical activity with a low-calorie diet results in greater weight loss and a greater reduction in abdominal fat than diet or physical activity alone. However, inducing an obese and chronically sedentary person to practice constant aerobic-type physical activity is one of the most difficult tasks for the physician facing an obese patient.

Moreover, the patient is not always in a position to carry out any aerobic exercise, even of low intensity. The obesity we are facing is frequently associated with various complications of metabolic and cardiovascular, but also respiratory and osteo-type. This severely limits the possibility and ability of the obese patient to perform even the slightest aerobic exercise. It is therefore of fundamental importance to set up a short and long-term strategy to try to promote a radical but continuous change in lifestyle. In the planning of the exercise, it is necessary to take into account the intensity, duration, and frequency, to produce progressive adaptation phenomena to progressively improve the tolerability to exercise. Before starting any type of activity, it is necessary to carry out a clinical evaluation to be able to set up targeted programs adapted to the degree of obesity, age, and overall clinical picture. In this way, it will be possible to plan various activities according to the cases and according to defined programs, chosen according to the characteristics of the individual subject. Taking into account the degree of obesity and the complications present, it is possible to recommend a physical activity to be carried out in three different areas:

- working in the water where the execution of movements is facilitated by the thrust of the water, which allows you to perform soft and intense exercises, but above all to perform great excursions to the benefit of the osteoarticular districts and the lengthening of the muscles, obtaining an initial strengthening of the limbs. Everything can also be done using small tools and elastic resistances.

  - The work in the gym should be specially equipped to use machinery appropriate to the patient obese. In particular, you can use specific treadmills - roulants (Cardio-Run), classic and reclined bikes (classic and horizontal Cycloergometer), with wide seats and backs, to maintain an adequate posture during exercise, arm - cycling (Top) and, in some cases, perform exercises with the Synchro. All exercises should be performed with heart rate monitoring trying not to exceed the aerobic threshold, and then working at a maximum oxygen consumption (VO2 max) < 70% of the maximum (usually VO2 max between 40-65% of the maximum), calculated according to the Karvonen formula [(FCMax-FCRip)+FCRip x load percentage]. Exercises should be interspersed with personalized activities of stretching, and/or aerobic activities, in some cases, conducted with a modest weight load applied to the limbs.

- Outdoor exercise, which can begin with a walk of variable and incremental duration that should contribute to improving the functionality and tolerability of the movement of the obese patient. The intensity of the movement is gradually increased once the full correctness of the movement is reached. It is preferable to perform the movement on flat paths so as not to increase the possibility of an injury.

When doing physical activity, the patient should be recommended to monitor physical activity with a diary (self-monitoring).

Physical activity should have some important requirements:
- In elderly subjects or those who have cardiovascular risk factors, a preliminary cardiological evaluation should be carried out.
- Initially, 30 to 45 minutes of aerobic exercise should be recommended three times a week.
- A moderate and gradual increase should be encouraged as the initial workload may be excessive for the overweight patient.

- A short, high-intensity job is not useful for weight loss, because it is quickly tired and does not effectively affect energy expenditure: the energy substrates used with this intensity come only marginally from fat and mostly from muscle and liver glycogen.
- The ideal work intensity for fat burning is a low intensity, within the aerobic threshold, between 60 and 70% of one's maximum heart rate. (With these measures you get a slight increase in muscle tone and cardiovascular adaptation).
- To improve the quality and speed of weight loss, aerobic work can be supplemented with anaerobic muscle-building activity, especially in large muscle groups. (With an increase in muscle mass there is a significant increase in the basal metabolic rate, thus increasing the burning capacity of the body's energy reserves).

To clarify the idea of the influence of physical exercise on the quality of life, we can observe that the daily caloric expenditure depends on three components such as:

- Basal metabolism (60-75%)
- food-induced thermogenesis (5-10%)
- physical activity (15-30%)

Exercise is, therefore, the easiest way to voluntarily increase calorie consumption, which is influenced by the type, intensity, and duration of the exercise.

The long-term benefits of aerobic physical activity include improving the capacity to transport and use oxygen during exercise, reducing blood pressure, and improving body composition.

Aerobic physical activity determines an improvement in the cardiovascular risk profile with mechanisms that are partly direct and partly consequent to weight loss.

Obesity, in particular, visceral obesity, is frequently associated with the presence of the metabolic syndrome to which a state of insulin resistance contributes decisively.

Aerobic exercise is a sure way to improve insulin sensitivity, independently of other interventions.

The American College of Sports Medicine and the American Diabetes Association indicate that physical activity (mainly aerobic) is one of the most important therapeutic means for the prevention and treatment of type 2 diabetes mellitus.

The improvement in insulin-sensitivity resulting from increased physical activity, regardless of diet, is associated with the improvement of additional parameters such as blood pressure, HDL cholesterol, and triglycerides.

Numerous studies have shown that aerobic exercise, of medium intensity and carried out continuously (about 1 hour a day with VO2 max 60-70%), can reduce insulin resistance and increase the consumption of oxygen at the level of the muscle fiber.

Even a continuous exercise of low intensity (50% of VO2 max), such as walking at a fast pace, has a positive effect not only on energy expenditure and body composition but directly on the metabolic profile, with the improvement of all cardiovascular risk factors.

Anaerobic exercise, carried out continuously, can prevent the onset of hypertension and reduce the values of resting PA through a direct mechanism, regardless of weight loss.

Aerobic physical activity is, therefore, a model of behavior to be recommended to all hypertensive patients, adapting the type and intensity according to the degree of impairment of the target organs.

The main mechanisms through which regular physical exercise can reduce PA values are represented by a reduction in sympathetic tone, an increase in the muscular vascular bed, and an increase in arterial compliance.

Secondary mechanisms are sodium loss and plasma volume reduction related to sweating.

The benefits of exercise on blood pressure are observed in hypertension rather than in normotension, in all ages and ethnic groups, both obese and normal weight.

Two types of physical activity are not indicated in the hypertensive patient: isometric activity, i.e. weighing with high loads, and apnea.

In the former, the contraction of all muscles, including the respiratory ones, with the consequent activation of SNS is not balanced, as in dynamic physical activity, by the vasodilatation of the muscles in exercise.

Therefore, in isometric-type physical activity, there is also an increase in diastolic blood pressure due to an increase in peripheral resistance.

Apnea represents a model of abnormal activation of SNS following various stimuli.

Therefore, when asked whether all obese patients can and/or must perform physical activity, the answer is certainly affirmative.

Physical exercise and weight reduction

Numerous studies have shown the beneficial effects of weight and body fat reduction in people with overweight or obesity. The use of exercise in the therapeutic management of excess weight is essential. The achievement of a weight loss is closely linked to achieving a negative energy balance and the more negative it is, the more weight loss will be. Since it is generally necessary to achieve an energy deficit of 500-1000 kcal/day (2000-4000 KJ) to reduce body weight by 0.5-1.0 kg per week, it is extremely difficult to achieve a deficit of this magnitude only with the practice of motor activity.

Physical activity levels achieved in military training or sports such as high-altitude mountaineering can result in significant weight loss; however, for most individuals, it is difficult to achieve and sustain these high levels of activity. Among the studies that evaluated the effects of using physical activity as the only tool to achieve weight loss in overweight-obese and sedentary individuals, few have demonstrated a significant weight reduction, i.e. greater than or equal to 3% of the baseline weight; and in a few studies "a dose" of physical activity sufficient to produce a significant weight loss was achieved. In most obese individuals, therefore, additional interventions (energy restriction or low-calorie diet) are necessary, in addition to physical exercise, to achieve a significant weight reduction. A systematic review of randomized controlled trials indicated that the treatment that produced the greatest weight loss was the one that included physical activity, diet, and behavioral therapy. The review also showed that the intensity of training should be moderate.

Studies in which the effects of less than 150 min per week of physical activity were evaluated did not show significant weight reductions.

A study in 2010 compared the effects of 90 min of moderate-intensity physical activity, performed continuously (30 minutes for 3 days a week), and 150 min of moderate-intensity, intermittent physical activity (30 min, 5 days a week), in women for 18 months. Although the group practicing continuous activity lost weight more significantly (1.7 vs. 0.8 kg), neither group lost more than 3% of its baseline weight.

In well-controlled and supervised laboratory studies, there is usually more weight loss; this may reflect a greater amount of supervised gym activity than unsupervised, independent activity. In fact, males and females who achieve a daily deficit of 500-700 kcal (2095-2933 KJ) for 12 weeks lost an average of 7.5 kg (8%) and 5.9 kg (6.5%), respectively.

Ultimately, any increase in physical activity levels is likely to have a potential effect on weight reduction, but in the light of current evidence, it appears that levels < 150 min per week do not significantly change weight, levels > 150 min lead to modest decreases. weight (2-3 kg) and levels between 225-420 result in 5-7.5 kg of weight loss; these effects underline the likely existence of a dose-response relationship.

The person overweight and obesity requires careful evaluation before starting a physical exercise program. Compared to the assessment required by an adult in good health, obesity due to frequent associated diseases (cardiovascular, respiratory, osteoarticular) requires a multidisciplinary approach involving different professional figures: internist, endocrinologist, cardiologist, and sports medicine specialist to assess the directions to the exercise test; orthopedist and physiotherapist to assess the impact of the exercise program on the osteoarticular apparatus. The individualized exercise program, agreed between these professionals, can then be guided by a graduate in motor sciences, preferably with a master's degree in adaptive and rehabilitative sciences, who have acquired specific skills in the field.

Exercise and maintaining weight loss

While the effects on weight reduction of physical exercise alone are minimal, the role played by physical activity in managing weight maintenance after weight loss is crucial. Physical activity is universally recommended for weight maintenance after a significant weight loss and the levels of physical activity performed are often referred to as the best predictor of weight maintenance after a significant weight loss.

An expenditure of 11-12 kcal/kg/day (46.1-50.3 KJ/kg/day) is necessary to pursue weight maintenance, while data from the National Weight Control Registry, where more than 3,000 individuals who have successfully achieved a weight loss of at least 13.5 kg for a minimum of 1 year are registered, indicate that a higher level of daily physical activity may be necessary to prevent weight recovery.

These individuals reported that they had used various methods to pursue weight loss and more than 90% emphasized, as crucial to long-term weight maintenance, the practice of high levels of physical activity.

All studies show that the practice of physical activity and weight recovery are inversely related and the higher the level of activity practiced the lower the amount of increase. The only 3 studies in which randomization to physical activity occurred after pursuing weight loss showed that physical activity has an indifferent effect, negative or positive, on the prevention of weight regain. Failure to randomize at different levels of physical activity after weight loss has been achieved is an important limit in assessing the effectiveness of physical activity after a period of weight loss. Although therefore, the role of physical activity in maintaining weight loss in obese subjects is indisputable, the amount needed remains uncertain, also considering that it can vary between individuals. Literature data specifies that at least 30 minutes of moderate physical activity should be performed for most days of the week, but the long-term maintenance of weight loss is linked to the performance of at least 200-300 minutes of activity per week.

Ultimately, about the use of physical activity for weight maintenance after a significant weight loss, most of the available literature indicates that "more is better". However, there are no specific, adequate, and sufficiently long-lasting studies, nor randomized, controlled clinical trials to specifically define the amount needed. Given these limitations, weight maintenance (<3% increase) can be associated with the practice of at least 60 minutes of walking per day (about 6 km) at moderate intensity.

Training programs for overweight/obese subjects

Obesity is frequently associated with various metabolic and cardiovascular complications, but also respiratory and osteoarticular complications, which severely limit the possibility and ability of the obese patient to perform even a minimal aerobic exercise. Before starting any type of activity, it is necessary to carry out a clinical evaluation to be able to set up targeted and adapted programs according to the degree of obesity, age, and overall clinical picture. In this way, it will be possible to plan various activities according to the cases and according to defined programs, chosen according to the characteristics of the individual subject. Moreover, the patient is not always in a position to carry out any type of aerobic exercise, even of low intensity.

Therefore, in the planning of the exercise, it is necessary to take into account the intensity, duration, and frequency, to produce progressive adaptation phenomena to progressively improve the tolerability to exercise.

Taking into account the degree of obesity and the complications present, it is possible to recommend a program of physical activity to be carried out in the water, in the gym, or the open air.

An example of training to be done to an obese person who arrives for the first time at the gym is shown below:

We start with a bike that can be reclined and with support or without support: the choice depends on the size of the subject, as can be deduced in a recline is difficult to pedal for a large obese subject because the abdomen comes into conflict with the knees and would force him to pedal with legs spread with a wrong posture. A recline, on the other hand, would be optimal in preventing back problems given the support of the back.

Continuing, we first make him do exercises of arm circumcisions in one direction and the other followed by squats (only hints) made with the help of a fitball leaning against the wall to protect the back. Another exercise to do is to make him twist his torso with a stick.

We continue by making him perform light traction to a special machine in which we can adjust the load to be lifted.

Finally, we move on to the treadmill followed by stretching exercises.

Subsequent types of training could be these:

- exercises on the ground on a mat on which to perform various types of exercises involving all muscle groups: these can be done with the free body, with the help of elastic ropes, fitballs, small dumbbells, etc. ....

- exercises performed on the back with the help of elastic ropes in which to seek control of movement and correct posture because there is the help of the machine to direct them.

The recovery time between one exercise and the next is hypothetically 2 minutes. The times, loads, and intensities of the exercises are only hypothetical and must be adapted from time to time and from subject to subject. The work of the following cards stimulates lipolysis and working also on the resistant force increases the basal metabolism.

Effects of physical activity on psychological well-being

The therapeutic objective is the recovery of the psycho-physical form of the patient, to promote a change in lifestyle and correction of habits that have contributed to the appearance of obesity. The psychological aspects connected to the development of obesity should not be underestimated.

It is important to give positive reinforcements:
- encourage the patient to verify the improvement of performance
- draw attention to the feeling of well-being after exercise
- highlight changes in body shape, regardless of weight changes

We must bear in mind the pursuit of pleasantness:
- take into account the patient's preferences regarding the type of exercise

- a type of exercise that is very pleasing to the patient is preferable to a less pleasing one

And also of sociality:

- compliance increases if the exercise is carried out together with someone else
- compliance increases if the exercise is carried out in a structured manner outside the home

And the gradualness of the objectives:

- start with light intensity programs and then increase progressively
- try to include even minor exercises in normal daily activities (going shopping on foot, not taking the elevator, etc.).

In support of the above, numerous literature data have for years supported a correlation between physical activity and psychopathology. Since 1896, the young Dr. O. Fache has been supporting a medical thesis:

The lack of activity can be a wake-up call for the beginning of depressive symptoms, which is often a component present in subjects with eating disorders. On the contrary, the sport seems to be associated with good mental health.

It is now established that physical exercise has a positive effect on psychopathology. There is now sufficient scientific evidence to support the idea that physical activity has significant effects on memory capacity, mental status, and dysfunctional eating habits. Physical activity seems to act by improving the feeling of effectiveness and self-confidence. This is done by still being able to set goals and thus increase self-efficacy. Polarization on physical activity can also represent a positive distraction that can also improve cognitive performance.

The physical improvement resulting from regular physical activity can help to increase self-esteem and encourage comparison with others by contrasting the tendency to social withdrawal in people suffering from obesity. The mechanism through which there is an improvement in mood is probably linked to the increase in endorphins and serotonin as an acute response to physical activity. Aerobic activity probably acts by increasing respiratory capacity. Our brain is sensitive to the variations that are recorded in the concentrations of carbon dioxide and oxygen; the balance between these two gases influences the one between the two neurotransmitters: gammamine butyric acid (GABA), which has an activity inhibiting brain activity, and glutamate, which would act as an exciter. An oxygen deficiency and a parallel increase in carbon dioxide could unbalance brain transmission in favor of GABA, with a depression of the brain and mental activity.

Therefore, better regulating our breathing capacity can have the effect of rebalancing nerve transmission and consequently mood. Other studies have instead shown a relationship of aerobic activity with the increase of noradrenaline, serotonin, and endorphins, all neuro mediators involved in anxiety disorders, phobias, and depression that are often found in subjects with eating disorders. In large obese subjects the antidepressant action of physical activity, even in the case of severe depression, is evident and documented after 10 days.

Antidepressants begin their activity after about 15 days from the beginning of intake. Physical activity in particular running acts even earlier.

The explanations for the results of this pilot study can be different: one can think of the fact that running (or, in any case, physical exercise) favors the production of some neurotransmitters that raise the level of mood, or of the fact that the metabolic action of exercise influences brain function.

New studies have since followed in confirming the positive effect on the mood of physical exercise in whatever way it is done.

An American study showed a significant improvement in mood, after 3 months, even in subjects who had done only flexibility exercises. In subjects who had engaged in more intensive activities, mood disorders were reduced by 50%.

According to the study, effectiveness, therefore, increases with the intensity of the exercise; this makes us understand how exercise can help obese people with eating disorders.

In a study carried out on 1122 university students from Mexico City in 2013, Lazarevich highlighted how important programs are for the development of correct eating habits and physical activity in the global approach to obesity; however, they must be supported by strategies for managing emotions, techniques for reducing impulsiveness and promoting a positive mood.

A study published in February 2014, was analyzed lifestyle changes in 100 obese subjects including a minimum of 90 minutes of adapted physical activity 5 days a week for 10/14 weeks. Quality of life was assessed by Binge Eating Scale, Hospital Anxiety and Depression Scale, and SF-36: a reduction in Binge Eating Disorder and depression and an increase in physical and mental health emerged compared to the control group. Improvements in Binge Eating Disorder and physical health have been associated with weight loss. Also at 6 and 12 months, there was a reduction in systolic blood pressure, blood sugar, triglycerides, and LDL cholesterol and an increase in that HDL.

7.Conclusions

The epidemic explosion of obesity has reached such a level that it has become one of the most important areas of intervention for the protection of public health for the World Health Organisation. The phenomenon is widespread to varying degrees in all regions of our country and its prevalence is constantly increasing, with a worrying expansion in childhood. In most cases, obesity is defined as essential or primitive and its onset is mainly due to environmental and genetic factors. Environmental factors include the reduction of individual energy expenditure, facilitated by sedentary work and poor exercise habits, and the increasing availability of food.

The objective of controlling and reducing the epidemic spread of obesity can be achieved through a comprehensive strategy using integrated actions, addressing the social, economic, and environmental determinants underlying individual behavior. The importance of a multidisciplinary approach should, therefore, be emphasized.

In particular, it is important to highlight the important role that physical activity plays in the prevention and treatment of obesity and the proven relationship between physical activity and eating disorders.

The alternation between aerobic and resistance work optimizes neuromuscular recruitment, improves fatigue tolerance, and reduces the risk of falls. It should also be borne in mind that mixed training is less monotonous and helps to improve motivation in these subjects. All this can allow us to plan long-term work with progressive objectives to be achieved and consolidated.

Numerous literature studies also show a clear causal association between continuous physical activity carried out in the manner reported and the improvement of dysfunctional eating habits. Surely the improvement of eating behavior is fundamental for weight loss and for maintaining the results achieved. It should also not be forgotten the fundamental role played by physical activity in the overall psychological well-being. As evidenced by several studies, obesity is often related to low self-esteem and depressive symptoms, and the physical exercise correctly performed is associated with an improvement in the quality of life through multiple mechanisms including the release of endorphins and other neurotransmitters in the brain.

Physical activity can, therefore, be considered a bit like a drug to be administered continuously to these subjects. This is surely one of our main tasks. The specialist in Motor Sciences must keep in mind that the planning of a program of physical activity adapted to the clinical picture of the subject is important as a prescription drug. Exercise, like a drug, can have beneficial effects not only on weight loss but also on the clinical picture and overall psychological well-being.

CPSIA information can be obtained
at www.ICGtesting.com
Printed in the USA
BVHW091009150521
607436BV00002B/515